THE BOOK OF QUESTIONS

GREGORY STOCK, PH.D.

EQUATION

First published 1987
by Workman Publishing Company, Inc.
1 West 39th Street, New York, NY 10018

First UK edition 1987

British Library Cataloguing in Publication Data

Stock, Gregory
The book of questions.
1. Self-realization — Problems, exercises,
etc.
I. Title
158'.1   BF637.S4

ISBN 1-85336-026-0

*Equation is an imprint of the
Thorsons Publishing Group Limited,
Denington Estate, Wellingborough, Northamptonshire,
NN8 2RQ, England*

Cover illustration: Tom Lulevitch

Printed in Great Britain by
Richard Clay, Bungay, Suffolk

1 3 5 7 9 10 8 6 4 2

To Mom and Dad,
for giving me the security to question
and the independence to seek my own answers.

ACKNOWLEDGEMENTS

I especially thank David Breznau, who thought of organizing questions of this sort into a book of questions. Without his contribution to the design and development of this book, it would not now exist.

I appreciate the assistance, encouragement, and support provided by Libby Anderson, Ann Cole, Steve Cole, Lorraine Campbell, Richard Campbell, Margarette Green, Al Jackson, Sandra Eugster, Ginny Mazur, Don Ponturo, Peter Trent, Fred Weber, and Arshad Zakaria. I am particularly grateful for the numerous thoughtful and valuable suggestions of my editor, Michael Cader.

I thank Claudia Summer for her many perceptive thoughts and comments; they were a big help in preserving and refining my vision of the book. Finally, I thank John Summer for our delightful brainstorming sessions on the questions. Many of the questions owe their origins to his fertile imagination.

INTRODUCTION

T his is not a book of trivia questions, so don't bother to look here for the name of either Tonto's horse or the shortstop for the 1923 Yankees. These are questions of a different sort—questions about you. They are about your values, your beliefs, and your life; love, money, sex, integrity, generosity, pride, and death are all here. Here is an enjoyable way to find out more about yourself and others, and to confront ethical dilemmas in a concrete rather than an abstract form. To respond to these questions, you will need to examine and interpret your past, project yourself into hypothetical situations, face difficult dilemmas, and make painful choices. These questions can be an avenue for individual growth, a tool for deepening relationships, a quick way to get to know a stranger, or merely a pleasant amusement.

These questions expose issues that warrant deep, solitary reflection, but also are particularly stimulating when explored with others. You will be surprised how effectively these questions catalyze unusual and rewarding discussions. A passing interaction with a woman in a café led me into an intoxicating five-hour tête-à-tête. A conversation with a long-standing friend gave me some valuable new insights about my life. A dull evening with some acquaintances was transformed into an exciting encounter lasting into the early-morning hours.

When conversing, we often exchange small talk without being very involved in our conversation; broach the questions here and see what happens. Start giving yourself permission to voice those dangerous questions you've never quite been willing to ask, those provocative thoughts whispered by an inner voice and soon forgotten. Too frequently we pull back from bringing up questions that seem awkward or intrusive, yet these are the very ones that will open paths to understanding and intimacy. When people encounter someone inquisitive who genuinely wants to hear what they have to say, far from being offended, they are usually eager to talk about the important things on their minds.

Enough different types of questions are posed here to enable you to identify both the subjects you shy away from and the ones you are drawn to. We react strongly to questions that touch our own unresolved conflicts, so the questions you avoid may be the ones you need to consider most. Are you fascinated by questions about health and mortality? Do you skip questions with a sexual slant? In this book successive questions probe unrelated issues, so whether you read pages in order or jump around, you will face unexpected topics. As you discuss these questions, keep in mind that the emotional tone and colour of a person's reply may communicate even more than the words themselves do.

There are no correct or incorrect answers to these questions, only honest or dishonest ones. Can you know what you would do in a strange hypothetical situation? Of course you can't, but why let that inhibit you? This is a chance to gain insights without actually living through the predicaments described. Let yourself be swept up in these situations so that you care about the choices you make. Resist the temptation to escape from a question by denying its reality or by coming up with some complication that obscures the basic issue. Ignore the paradoxes of time-travel and the impossibility of various magical powers. Accept that conditions are as described, that odds are accurate, that promises will be fulfilled, and furthermore, that you know this when you are making your decisions.

Don't simply answer "yes" or "no" to these questions—probe and explain your responses and pursue interesting tangents. Use the questions as a point of departure and give your imagination full rein as you play with the situations described. Take an active role in toying with the conditions presented by extending them, changing them, and expanding them. If you feel a question lacks detail or is unclear, make an assumption that will correct the problem. As you explore and challenge your values and the values of your friends, you may soon discover questioning has become much more than just an entertaining pastime.

*Selected questions are marked with an asterisk to indicate that corresponding follow-up questions can be found at the back of the book, starting on page 181.

THE
BOOK OF
QUESTIONS

1

For a person you loved deeply, would you be willing to move to a distant country knowing there would be little chance of seeing your friends or family again?

2

Do you believe in ghosts or evil spirits? Would you be willing to spend a night alone in a remote house that is supposedly haunted?

3

If you were to die this evening with no opportunity to communicate with anyone, what would you most regret not having told someone? Why haven't you told them yet?

4

If you could spend one year in perfect happiness but afterwards would remember nothing of the experience would you do so? If not, why not!*

5

If a new medicine were developed that would cure arthritis but cause a fatal reaction in 1 percent of those who took it, would you want it to be released to the public?

6

You discover your wonderful one-year-old child is, because of a mixup at the hospital, not yours. Would you want to exchange the child to try to correct the mistake?

7

Do you think that the world will be a better or a worse place 100 years from now?

8

Would you rather be a member of a world championship sports team or be the champion of an individual sport? Which sport would you choose?

9

Would you accept £1,000,000 to leave the country and never set foot in it again?*

10

Which sex do you think has it easier in our culture? Have you ever wished you were of the opposite sex?

11

You are given the power to kill people simply by thinking of their deaths and twice repeating the word "good-bye." People would die a natural death and no one would suspect you. Are there any situations in which you would use this power?*

12

If you were able to live to the age of 90 and retain either the body or the mind of a 30-year-old for the last 60 years of your life, which would you want?

13

What would constitute a "perfect" evening for you?

14

Would you rather be extremely successful professionally and have a tolerable yet unexciting private life, or have an extremely happy private life and only a tolerable and uninspiring professional life?*

15

Whom do you admire most? In what way does that person inspire you?

16

If at birth you could select the profession your child would eventually pursue, would you do so?

17

Would you be willing to become extremely ugly physically if it meant you would live for 1,000 years at any physical age you chose?*

18

If you could wake up tomorrow having gained any one ability or quality, what would it be?

19

You have the chance to meet someone with whom you can have the most satisfying love imaginable—the stuff of dreams. Sadly, you know that in six months the person will die. Knowing the pain that would follow, would you still want to meet the person and fall in love? What if you knew your lover would not die, but instead would betray you?*

20

If you knew of a way to use your estate, following your death, to greatly benefit humanity, would you do it and leave only a minimal amount to your family?

21

Do you prefer being around men or women?
Do your closest friends tend to be men or
women?

22

If you could use a voodoo doll to hurt anyone
you chose, would you?

23

While on a trip to another city, your spouse (or lover) meets and spends a night with an exciting stranger. Given that they will never meet again, and that you will not otherwise learn of the incident, would you want your partner to tell you about it? If roles were reversed, would you reveal what you had done?*

24

Are there people you envy enough to want to trade lives with them? Who are they?

25

For an all-expense-paid, one-week holiday any-where in the world, would you be willing to kill a beautiful butterfly by pulling off its wings? What about stepping on a cockroach?*

26

Would you be willing to murder an innocent person if it would end hunger in the world?*

27

If God appeared to you in a series of vivid and moving dreams and told you to leave everything behind, travel alone to the Red Sea and become a fisherman, what would you do? What if you were told to sacrifice your child?

28

What is your most treasured memory?

29

Have you ever hated anyone? If so, why and for how long?

30

Would you rather be given £10,000 for your own use or £100,000 to give anonymously to strangers? What if you could keep £1,000,000 or give away £2,000,000?

31

If you knew there would be a nuclear war in one week, what would you do?

32

Would you accept twenty years of extraordinary happiness and fulfillment if it meant you would die at the end of the period?

33

What is the greatest accomplishment of your life? Is there anything you hope to do that is even better?

34

What was your most enjoyable dream? your worst nightmare?

35

Would you give up half of what you now own for a pill that would permanently change you so that one hour of sleep each day would fully refresh you?*

36

If you knew you could devote yourself to any single occupation—music, writing, acting, business, politics, medicine, etc.—and be among the best and most successful in the world at it, what would you choose? If you knew you had only a 10 percent chance of being so successful, would you still put in the effort?

37

What was your best experience with drugs or alcohol? your worst experience?

38

If you went to a dinner party and were offered a dish you had never tried, would you want to taste it even if it sounded strange and not very appealing?

39

Do your close friends tend to be older or younger than you?*

40

If the person you were engaged to marry had an accident and became a paraplegic, would you go through with the marriage or back out of it?

41

Your house, containing everything you own, catches fire; after saving your loved ones and pets, you have time to safely make a final dash to save any one item. What would it be?

42

How would you react if you were to learn that your mate had had a lover of the same sex before you knew each other?*

43

When were you last in a fight? What caused it and who won?

44

You are offered £1,000,000 for the following act: Before you are ten pistols — only one of which is loaded. You must pick up one of the pistols, point it at your forehead, and pull the trigger. If you can walk away you do so a millionaire. Would you accept the risk?

45

Someone very close to you is in pain, paralyzed, and will die within a month. He begs you to give him poison so that he can die. Would you? What if it were your father?*

46

When did you last sing to yourself? to someone else?

47

You have the power to go any distance into the future and, after one year, return to the present with any knowledge you have gained from your experience but with no physical objects. Would you make the journey if it carried a 50 percent risk of death?

48

Given the choice of anyone in the world, whom would you want as your dinner guest? as your close friend? as your lover?*

49

While parking late at night, you slightly scrape the side of a Porsche. You are certain no one else is aware of what happened. The damage is minor and would not be covered by insurance. Would you leave a note?

50

If you could choose the manner of your death, what would it be?*

51

Do you have any specific long-term goals? What is one and how do you plan on reaching it?*

52

For what in your life do you feel most grateful?

53

How do you react when people sing "Happy Birthday" to you in a restaurant?

54

What is the worst psychological torture you can imagine suffering? Anything causing even minor physical injury should not be considered.

55

Would you like your spouse to be both smarter and more attractive than you?

56

If you found that a good friend had AIDS, would you avoid him? What if your brother or sister had it?

57

Would you be willing to give up sex for one year if you knew it would give you a much deeper sense of peace than you have now?

58

A good friend pulls off a well-conceived practical joke that plays on one of your foibles and makes you look ridiculous. How would you react?*

59

By controlling medical research funds, you are in the position to guarantee that a cure will be found in 15 years for any disease you choose. Unfortunately, no progress on any others would be made during that period. Would you target one disease?

60

Would you add one year to your life if it meant taking one year from the life of someone in the world selected at random? Would it matter if you were told whose life you had shortened?

61

Can you urinate in front of another person?

62

If you walked out of your house one morning and saw a bird with a broken wing huddled in some nearby bushes, what would you do?

63

Assume there were a technological break-through that would allow people to travel as easily and cheaply between continents as between nearby cities. Unfortunately, there would also be 100,000 deaths a year from the device. Would you try to prevent its use?*

64

You and a person you love deeply are placed in separate rooms with a button next to each of you. You know that you will both be killed unless one of you presses your button before 60 minutes pass; furthermore, the first to press the button will save the other person, but will immediately be killed. What do you think you would do?

65

When you tell a story, do you often exagger-
ate or embellish it? If so, why?

66

Do you feel that advice from older people
carries a special weight because of their
greater experience?*

67

Without your kidney as a transplant, someone close to you will die within one month.
The odds that you will survive the operation
are only 50 percent, but should you survive
you would be certain of a normal life expectancy. Would you consent to the operation?*

68

When has your life dramatically changed as the result of some seemingly random external influence? How much do you feel in control of the course of your life?*

69

If a friend were almost always late, would you resent it or simply allow for it? Can you be counted on to be on time?

70

When did you last yell at someone? Why? Did you later regret it?

71

Would you be willing to have horrible night-mares every night for a year if you would be rewarded with extraordinary wealth?*

72

If you could have free, unlimited service for five years from an extremely good cook, chauffeur, housekeeper, masseuse, or personal secretary, which would you choose?

73

Would you be willing to go to a slaughter-house and kill a cow? Do you eat meat?

74

Would you enjoy spending a month of solitude in a beautiful natural setting? Food and shelter would be provided but you would not see another person.

75

After a medical examination, your doctor calls and gravely says you have a rare lymphatic cancer and only a few months to live. Five days later, she informs you that the lab tests were mislabelled; you are perfectly healthy. Forced for a moment to look death in the face, you have been allowed to turn and go on. During those difficult days you would certainly have gained some insights about yourself. Do you think they would be worth the pain?

76

One hot summer afternoon, while walking through a parking lot at a large shopping centre, you notice a dog suffering badly from the heat inside a locked car. What would you do?

77

Do you feel ill at ease going alone to either dinner or the cinema? What about going on a holiday by yourself?

78

If you knew that in one year you would die suddenly, would you change anything about the way you are now living?

79

For £20,000 would you go for three months without washing, brushing your teeth, or using deodorant? Assume you could not explain your reasons to anyone.

80

Would you rather die peacefully among friends at age 50, or painfully and alone at age 80? Assume that most of the last 30 years would be good ones.

81

If you were to discover that your closest friend was a heroin dealer, what would you do?

82

Is it easy for you to accept help when you need it? Will you ask for help?

83

If you were helping to raise money for a charity and someone agreed to make a large contribution if you would perform at the upcoming fund-raising show, would you? If so, what would you like to perform? Assume the show would have an audience of about 1,000.

84

Would you have one of your fingers surgically removed if it somehow guaranteed immunity from all major diseases?

85

Would you like to be famous? In what way?

86

How do you picture your funeral? Is is important for you to have people mourn your death?*

87

Would you accept a job twice as good as your present one — twice as much money and twice as fulfilling — given one condition of employment: you can never reveal anything about it to anyone you know?

88

You, your closest friend, and your father are on holiday together, hiking in a remote jungle. Your two companions stumble into a nest of poisonous vipers and are bitten repeatedly. You know neither will live without an immediate shot of anti-venom, yet there is only a single dose of anti-venom and it is in your pocket. What would you do?

89

Where would you choose to be if you could place yourself anywhere on a scale from one to ten, where one is hardship, struggle, and extraordinary accomplishment and ten is comfort, peace of mind, and no accomplishment. Why? Where are you now?

90

If you could choose the sex and physical appearance of your soon-to-be-born child, would you do it?*

91

Would you rather play a game with someone more or less talented than you? Would it matter who was watching?

92

Is there something you've dreamed of doing for a long time? Why haven't you done it?*

93

While in the government, you discover the Prime Minister is commiting extortion and other serious crimes. By exposing the situation you might bring about the Prime Minister's downfall, but your career would be destroyed because you would be framed, fired, and publicly humiliated on other matters. Knowing you would be vindicated five years later, would you blow the whistle? What if you knew you would never be vindicated?

94

On a busy street you are approached apologetically by a well-dressed stranger who asks for a pound to catch a bus and make a phone call. He says he has lost his wallet. What would you do? If approached in the same way by a haggard-looking stranger claiming to be hungry and unable to find a job, what would you do?

95

If by sacrificing your life you could contribute so much to the world that you would be honoured in all nations, would you be willing to do so? If so, would you make the same sacrifice knowing that someone you thoroughly disliked would receive the honour while you went unrecognized?

96

Knowing you had a 50 percent chance of winning and would be paid 10 times the amount of your bet if you won, what fraction of what you now own would you be willing to wager?

97

What are your most compulsive habits? Do you regularly struggle to break these habits?

98

You know you will die of an incurable disease within three months. Would you allow yourself to be frozen within the week if you knew it would give you a modest chance of being revived in 1,000 years and living a greatly extended life?

99

You are driving late at night in a safe but deserted neighbourhood when a dog suddenly darts in front of your car. Though you slam on the brakes, you hit the animal. Would you stop to see how injured the animal was? If you did so and found that the dog was dead but had a name tag, would you contact the owner?

100

What do you most strive for in your life: accomplishment, security, love, power, excitement, knowledge, or something else?

101

An eccentric millionaire offers to donate a large sum to charity if you will step— completely naked—from a car onto a busy city street, walk two hundred yards, and climb back into the car. Knowing that there would be no danger of physical abuse, would you do it?*

102

How close and warm is your family? Do you feel your childhood was happier than most other people's?*

103

Does the fact that you have never done something before increase or decrease its appeal to you?

104

Would you be willing to give up sex for five years if you could have wonderfully sensual and erotic dreams any night you wished?

105

At a meal, your friends start belittling a common acquaintance. If you felt their criticisms were unjustified, would you defend the person?

106

Do you usually make a special effort to thank someone who does you a favour? How do you react when you aren't thanked for going out of your way for someone?

107

Would you like to have your rate of physical ageing slowed by a factor of thirty so as to give you a life expectancy of about 2,000 years?*

108

You are invited to a party that will be attended by many fascinating people you've never met. Would you want to go if you had to go by yourself?

109

Since adolescence, in what three-year period do you feel you experienced the most personal growth and change?

110

If you were having difficulty on an important test and could safely cheat by looking at someone else's paper, would you do so?*

111

If your parents became infirm and the only alternative to bringing them into your home was to put them in a nursing home, would you do so? What about a sister or brother who suffered a permanently crippling injury and—other than your home—had nowhere to go but a convalescent home?

112

Forced to choose between the following two legal systems, which would you select? With one, the guilty are always convicted, but each month 1 innocent person is mistakenly punished. With the other, the innocent are always acquitted, but each month 5 guilty criminals are mistakenly released.

113

If you could take a one-month trip anywhere in the world and money were not a consideration, where would you go and what would you do?

114

Would you be willing to reduce your life expectancy by five years to become extremely attractive?

115

Given the ability to project yourself into the past but not return, would you do so? Where would you go and what would you try to accomplish if you knew you might change the course of history?*

116

How many different sexual partners have you had in your life? Would you prefer to have had more or fewer?

117

Have you ever considered suicide? What is so important to you that without it life would not be worth living?

118

If your friends and acquaintances were willing to bluntly and honestly tell you what they really thought of you, would you want them to?*

119

If this country were to suffer an unprovoked nuclear attack and would be totally obliterated in a matter of minutes, would you favour unleashing the NATO nuclear arsenal upon the attackers?

120

Would you accept £10,000 to shave your head and continue your normal activities sans hat or wig without explaining the reason for your haircut?

121

Were you able to wake up tomorrow in the body of someone else, would you do so? Whom would you pick?

122

If you were happily married, and then met someone you felt was certain to always bring you deeply passionate, intoxicating love, would you leave your spouse? What if you had children?

123

When you do something ridiculous, how much does it bother you to have other people notice it and laugh at you?

124

Who is the most important person in your life? What could you do to improve the relationship? Will you ever do it?

125

Assuming that complete recovery were instantaneous, would you be willing to accept a year of complete paralysis below the neck to prevent the otherwise certain extinction of the blue whale?*

126

Do you believe in capital punishment? Would you be willing to execute a man sentenced to death by the courts if you were selected by lot to do so and he would go free if you refused? Assume you know no details of the trial.

127

If you could change anything about the way you were raised, what would it be?*

128

If a flying saucer arrived and aliens invited you to visit their planet for 5 years, would you go? If instead they gave you no choice and forced you to join them permanently, what would you bring with you if allowed to take a trunk filled with anything you wanted?

129

Do you believe in any sort of God? If not, do you think you might still pray if you were in a life-threatening situation?

130

While out one day, you are surprised to see
your mother holding hands with someone
who is clearly her lover. She notices you,
runs over, and begs you not to say anything
to your father. How would you respond?
What would you do if your father later told
you that he was going crazy because he kept
thinking your mother was having an affair yet
knew it was just his imagination?

131

If 100 people your age were chosen at random, how many do you think you'd find leading a more satisfying life than yours?

132

If you went to a beach and it turned out to be a nude beach, would you stay and go swimming? Would you swim nude?*

133

Have you had satisfying sex within the last three months?

134

Would it disturb you much if, upon your death, your body were simply thrown into the woods and left to rot? Why?

135

Which would you prefer: a wild, turbulent life filled with joy, sorrow, passion, and adventure—intoxicating successes and stunning setbacks; or a happy, secure, predictable life surrounded by friends and family without such wide swings of fortune and mood?

136

If you knew your child would be severely retarded and would die by the age of five, would you decide to have an abortion?*

137

Do you find it so hard to say "no" that you regularly do favours you do not want to do? If so, why?

138

If you began to be very attracted to someone of another race, how would your behaviour differ from what it would be towards someone of your own race?

139

Would you rather spend a month on holiday with your parents or put in overtime at your current job for four weeks without extra compensation?

140

Would you like to know the precise date of your death?*

141

Would you accept a guaranteed, lifetime allowance of £50,000 per year (adjusted annually for inflation) if accepting it meant that you could never again earn money from either work or investments?*

142

What, if anything, is too serious to be joked about?

143

Do you ever spit or pick your nose in public? What about cleaning your teeth with a tooth-pick?

144

A close friend asks—and genuinely wants—your opinion about something, but your opinion is one that he is likely to find quite painful. For example, your friend is an artist and asks your honest estimate of his chances of being successful. You think he is an atrocious artist who hasn't the slightest chance of success. What would you do?

145

Do you have a favourite sexual fantasy? Would you like to have it fulfilled?

146

If you knew a thermonuclear holocaust would occur in precisely 20 years and no one would survive it, how would you change your present life?

147

When did you last cry in front of another person? by yourself?

148

If, by having a 2 inch by 2 inch tattoo, you could save five lives and prevent a terrorist attack, would you do so? If you were allowed to select the location and design, where would you have it and what would the design be?

149

Someone you love deeply is brutally murdered and you know the identity of the murderer, who unfortunately is acquitted of the crime. Would you seek revenge?

150

Would you be willing to give up all television for the next five years if it would induce someone to provide for 1,000 starving children in Ethiopia?*

151

While arguing with a close friend on the telephone, she gets angry and hangs up. Assuming she is at fault and makes no attempt to contact you, how long would you wait to get in touch with her?

152

What do you value most in a relationship?

153

If you learned you would die in a few days, what regrets would you have? Were you given five extra years of life, could you avoid those same regrets five years hence?*

154

Do you judge others by higher or lower standards than you use to judge yourself?

155

Would you be willing to make a substantial sacrifice to have any of the following: your picture on a postage stamp, your statue in a park, a college named after you, a Nobel prize, a national holiday in your honour?*

156

On an aeroplane you are talking pleasantly to a stranger of average appearance. Unexpectedly, the person offers you £10,000 for one night of sex. Knowing that there is no danger and that payment is certain, would you accept the offer?*

157

If you had to spend the next two years inside a small but fully provisioned Antarctic shelter with one other person, whom would you like to have with you?

158

You notice a self-destructive behaviour pattern in a friend who is clearly unaware of it. Would you point it out?

159

If you had the choice of one intimate soulmate and no other close friends, or of no such soulmate and many friends and acquaintances, which would you choose?

160

You become involved romantically but after six months realize you need to end the relationship. If you were certain the person would commit suicide if you were to leave and were also certain you could not be happy with the person, what would you do?

161

If you wanted to look very sexy, how would you dress?

162

For £2,000 would you be willing to stand up in a crowded restaurant and, for at least a minute, loudly berate a waitress for some trivial imperfection in the service? If not, consider how grateful the waitress would be if you did so and later split the money with her.

163

If there were a public execution on television, would you watch it?

164

If someone offered you a large amount of money for some information about one of your company's products, would you accept it? Assume you know you won't be discovered.*

165

Do you consider yourself well organized?
How often do you have to look for your
keys?

166

If you could increase your I.Q. by forty
points by having an ugly scar stretching from
your mouth to your eye, would you do so?

167

Would you be willing to do something very unsatisfying (for example, clean toilets) for five years if you were certain that the experience would afterwards bring you a deep sense of personal fulfillment for the rest of your life?

168

What things are too personal to discuss with others?

169

How many times during the day do you look at yourself in the mirror?

170

Walking along an empty street, you notice a wallet. It contains £5,000 in cash but no name or address. What would you do? Would it alter your decision if inside you found the name, address, and picture of either a wealthy-looking young man or a frail-looking old woman?*

171

Would you prefer to be blind or deaf?

172

Would you be content with a marriage of the highest quality in all respects but one—it completely lacked sex?*

173

When was the last time you stole something?
Why haven't you stolen anything since then?

174

How many of your friendships have lasted more than ten years? Which of your current friends do you feel will still be important to you ten years from now?

175

If you could mould to your liking your memories of any past experience, would you do so?

176

Before making a telephone call, do you ever rehearse what you are going to say?

177

How old were you when you first had sexual intercourse?*

178

You are leading 100 people whose lives are in danger and you must choose between two courses of action. One would save only 90 people; the other would have a 50 percent chance of saving everyone but were it to fail everyone would die. Which would you choose?*

179

Would you rather live in a democracy where leaders are usually either incompetent or dishonest, or in a dictatorship where leaders are generally talented and well-meaning?

180

For £1,000,000 would you be willing to never again see or talk to your best friend?*

181

What do you like best about your life? least?

182

Have you ever disliked someone for being luckier or more successful than you?

183

A cave-in occurs while you and a stranger are in a concrete room deep in a mine shaft. Before the phone goes dead, you learn the entire mine is sealed and the air hole being drilled will not reach you for 30 hours. If you both take sleeping pills from the medicine chest, the oxygen will last for only 20 hours. Both of you can't survive; alone, one of you might. After you both realize this, the stranger takes several sleeping pills, says that it is in God's hands, and falls asleep. You have a pistol; what do you do?

184

When you are given a compliment do you usually acknowledge it or suggest that you really do not deserve it?

185

What sorts of things would you do if you could be as outgoing and uninhibited as you wished? Do you usually initiate friendships or wait to be approached?

186

If you decided to do something and your friends strongly advised you not to, could you do it anyway?

187

In a nice restaurant, after getting the bill for an excellent meal, you notice that you were not charged for one of the items you ate. Would you tell the waitress?

188

Do you establish routines in your life? For example, do you usually sleep in the same place in your bed? eat meals at the same time? regularly return to the same holiday destination?

189

Can you be counted on to do what you say you'll do? What does it take for you to trust someone?

190

Do you feel you have much impact on the lives of people you come in contact with? Can you think of someone who, over a short period of time, significantly influenced your life?

191

Would you rather be happy yet slow-witted and unimaginative or unhappy yet bright and creative? For example, would you rather live the life of a brilliant yet tortured artist such as Vincent van Gogh, or that of a happy but carefree soul who is a bit simple-minded?

192

When you are with your friends, do your interactions include much touching—for example, hugging, kissing, roughhousing, or rubbing backs? Would you like to have more of this?

193

Given the ability to project yourself into the future but not return, would you do so? If not, would you change your mind if you could take someone along? How far would you go?*

194

Would you generally rather be overdressed or underdressed at a party?

195

Of all the people close to you, whose death would you find most disturbing?

196

You have arranged an evening with a friend, but on the day preceding your date a special opportunity arises to do something much more exciting. How would you handle the situation?

197

What has been your biggest disappointment in life? your biggest failure?

198

If you could pass your whole life cared for in every way as you slumbered peacefully, entranced by wonderful dreams, would you do so?

199

You are given £1,000,000 to donate anonymously to charity or to a stranger. How would you dispose of it?

200

In conversations, do you tend to listen or talk more?*

201

Do you frequently find yourself—just to be polite—saying things you don't mean? For example, when you say good-bye to someone who does not interest you, do you act as though you enjoyed their company?

202

Would you be willing to commit perjury for a close friend? For example, might you testify that he was driving carefully when he hit a pedestrian even though he had been joking around and not paying attention?

203

Relative to the population at large, how do you rate your physical attractiveness? your intelligence? your personality?

204

What drugs have you tried for recreational purposes? Are there any (for example, hashish, opium, cocaine, LSD, heroin, etc.) you would enjoy trying given the opportunity to do so in a nice setting where the drugs were legally provided by a physician? What appeals to you about such drugs? What are your major fears about taking them? Are you worried about physical or psychological damage? about addiction? about loss of control? about your values or character somehow being altered by the experience?

205

If you could prevent either an earthquake in Peru that would kill 40,000 people, a crash at your local airport that would kill 200 people, or an automobile accident that would kill an acquaintance of yours, which would you choose?

206

Would you be willing to eat a bowl of live grasshoppers for £40,000?

207

Do you enjoy sleeping in physical contact with your lover?

208

If you came upon the scene of a terrible road accident just after the ambulances arrived, would you stop to watch? Assume that your presence would neither help nor hinder the rescuers.

209

If you could script the basic plot for the dream you will have tonight, what would the story be?

210

You are given a chance to return to any previous point in your life and change a decision you made, but you will lose every thing that has happened to you since then. Is there a time you would return to? If so, would you like to retain the memory of the life you are giving up even though you could never recapture it?

211

Would £50,000 be enough money to induce you to take a loyal, healthy pet to the vet to be put to sleep?

212

You catch a rare immune disease and can survive only by remaining isolated inside a small sterilized room for the remainder of your life. Fortunately, you will have access to anything you want: books, music, tools, etc. Could you adjust to such a life and if so how would you spend your time?

213

What would you like to be doing five years from now? What do you think you will be doing five years from now?

214

What important decision in your professional life have you based largely upon your intuitive feelings? What about in your personal life?

215

Would you like to be elected Prime Minister of this country? Why? If so, would you still choose to be Prime Minister if it meant that your sleep would always be very fitful and disturbed, punctuated by frequent nightmares?

216

Assuming that you had no children and felt the only way for you to have a family was to marry someone you didn't love, would you be willing to do so?

217

If a crystal ball would tell you the truth about any one thing you wished to know concerning yourself, life, the future, or anything else, what would you want to know?

218

If you were guaranteed honest responses to any three questions, who would you question and what would you ask?

FURTHER
QUESTIONS

ow nice it would be to provide answers at this point; but personal questions such as these have no universal answers. Since each answer is a reflection of individual personality and experience, to evaluate our own responses we must look into ourselves. As with the initial questions, the object of the questions in this section is not to settle things with an "answer," but to go wherever the questions lead us. Though designed to be used in conjunction with the corresponding questions in the front of the book, this section can also be read and used independently. These follow-up questions suggest additional areas for reflection, and illustrate the process of probing and extending the original questions. Good questions don't lead to answers, they lead to more questions.

4

Which is more important: actual experiences, or the memories that remain when the experiences are over?

9

If you were expelled from the country and had only limited financial resources, where would you try to rebuild your life?

11

If you can imagine yourself killing someone indirectly, could you still see doing so if you had to look into the person's eyes and stab the person to death? Have you ever genuinely wanted to kill someone, or wished someone dead?

14

Since so many place great emphasis on a happy private life, why do people often wind up putting more energy into their professional lives? If you feel your private life is more important to you, do your priorities support this? Are you simply unwilling to admit that work is more important? Do you use work as a substitute? Do you hope professional success will somehow magically lead to personal happiness?

17

How much are you affected by a person's physical appearance? How would it change your life if something happened to make you much less attractive than you are now?

Do you find anything disturbing about immortality? What age seems ideal to you?

19

In love, is intensity or permanence more important to you? How much do you expect from someone who loves you? What would make you feel betrayed by your mate—indifference? dishonesty? infidelity?

23

How serious would an affair need to be before you would want and expect to be told about it? What makes hearing such a confession so threatening that most people would rather be deceived? Is this kind of honesty more likely to be destructive or to lead to greater intimacy and trust? How much do you trust your lover? How much can you be trusted?

25

Why does a beautiful creature merit more compassion than an ugly one? Does it damage us psychologically when we destroy something we find beautiful?

How meaningful is the difference between pulling the wings off an insect and stepping on it? Is the decision of how to kill something a minor decision when balanced against the decision of whether or not to kill it at all?

26

Would it torment you more to have the blood of an innocent person on your hands or to know you let millions of people die? What do you think of people who achieve great things by compromising their principles?

Many are willing to give their own lives but not to take the life of another; is anything so important you would sacrifice your very soul for it?

35

Do you feel you have enough time? If not, what would give you that feeling? How much has your attitude about time changed as you've aged?

39

What kind of people do you like to spend time with? What do such people bring out in you that others do not? What can people learn about you by looking at your friends?

42

Have you ever been sexually attracted to someone of the same sex? to someone in your family? If so, how did you deal with it?

45

Should it be illegal to help a terminally-ill person to die? If someone is not dying but has chronic pain, should the person be allowed to commit suicide? What if the person is in emotional rather than physical pain?

48

What do you seek in a friend yet neither expect nor want in a lover? Are you attracted to people who are healthy for you to be around?

50

Would you prefer to die a hero's death, die a martyr to some great cause, die in a natural catastrophe, or die peacefully? Why is it so tempting to have death catch us in our sleep?

How do your feelings about death influence the way you lead your life?

51

How often do you step back and reflect upon the way you are living and where you are headed? In what way will reaching your goals make your life more satisfying?

58

How forgiving are you when your friends let you down?

63

In the mid 1800s, had you been able to look into the future and see that the automobile would cause 5 million fatalities in the next century, how would you have felt about this new device? Is there scientific knowledge that is best left undiscovered? If so, what areas of research do you feel should be restricted?

66

Do your comments and suggestions influence other people much? How could you present your ideas so that they would have more impact?

67

Would you risk your life for someone close to you out of feelings of obligation or out of feelings of love? Would it matter if you could refuse without anyone ever knowing? What if the person asked you not to risk your life?

68

Does living as though you control your own destiny lead to a more powerful life?

71

What would you do if you realized that unless you changed jobs and took a 25 percent pay cut, you would have moderate insomnia and a nightmare every month or so? Is there anything worse than the worst nightmare?

79

How do you react to the idea that more people are willing to have sex for money (question 156) than to forgo washing? A century ago this would not have been the case; do you think our more permissive sexual attitude is a healthy development? What about our increased attention to personal hygiene? How important is advertising in bringing about these changes?

86

How would you like to be remembered after you die? What would you like said at your funeral? Whom would you like to speak?

90

Would you like to have a child much brighter and more attractive than yourself? What difficulties might result? How much would it bother you to have an ugly, stupid, or crippled child? To ensure your baby would be born bright, attractive, and healthy, would you use a safe medical procedure to genetically alter the developing embryo? Would a baby designed in this way still feel like your child?

92

Is it better to have dreams that will never come to pass, or to have no dreams at all? How much better would your life be if the things you dream of doing or having were granted to you?

101

In terms of their relative unpleasantness, how would you rank the following: a nude stroll in public; being spat upon by a crowd of people; being arrested for shoplifting; begging for money at an airport? What is the most embarrassing thing you can imagine? What bothers you about looking bad in front of strangers?

102

Do you feel that children should be sheltered from unhappiness? What from your childhood has proved most valuable? most difficult to over-come?

107

How hard would it be to outlive and lose each person you grew close to? If you lived a greatly lengthened life, would you experience so much that you'd soon feel surrounded by children? Would you be able to adjust to the dramatic social changes? Would you soon grow jaded, feeling there was nothing interesting left?

Does feeling that life is too short increase the intensity and passion of it in a desirable way?

110

If you saw someone cheating on a test, what would you do? What if you had signed an honour code?

115

How might the world be different if you could actually change some historical event? How sure are you that the long-term consequences would be positive?

118

Do you think your friends would agree with one another about the kind of person you are? How much energy do you spend doing things to favourably impress other people? If you were completely unconcerned about what others would think, what sorts of things might you do? How do you feel when people like you because they think you are someone you are not?

125

When you make a big sacrifice, do you tell people about it or keep it to yourself? Do you feel

annoyed when your sacrifices aren't acknowl-
edged by others? What would you never willingly
sacrifice? your life? your health? your integrity?
your dreams?

127

In what ways will you treat (or have you treated)
your children differently from the way you were
treated? If you've already raised children and
could do it again knowing what you know now,
what would you do differently?

132

How much do you like your body? If you awoke
alone on a warm morning and were going to laze
around your home, how long would you wait to
get dressed? What do you wear when you sleep?

136

What are your feelings about killing a handicapped child at birth? Should a woman have the right to have an abortion for any reason she wants? What rights should the father have? If your 15-year-old sister became pregnant, would you want her to have an abortion? If you had a retarded baby, would you put the child in an institution?

140

How might knowing when you'll die help you plan your life? Is life enhanced by feeling that death could strike at any time? by not thinking about death at all? If you knew someone was dying, would you tell them the truth or deceive them about it? How many more years do you think you will live?

141

Would you accept a much less enjoyable job paying twice what you make now? If you received the same pay regardless of your job, what kind of work would you do? If you were financially independent, would you continue to work? If not, what would you do?

150

If giving up TV is too much of a sacrifice, would you consider switching to black-and-white viewing?

153

Can you envision how you are likely to look back upon the things you are doing today? If so, how much do you try to live now as you think you will one day wish you had lived?

155

Are honours more likely to come to those who seek them or to those who don't care about fame and think only of their work? How much do fame and accomplishment impress you? Does just knowing you've accomplished something worthwhile mean as much to you as getting attention and praise for the accomplishment?

156

Since so many people are willing to have sex for money, why is such a strong stigma attached to prostitution? Is there much difference between having sex for cash and having sex in the hope of getting some future benefit? Does the size of the payment alter the nature of the transaction?

164

How do you feel about taking a sick day at work when you aren't ill? Have you ever made unauthorized, personal, long-distance phone calls or taken tools or supplies from work? Have you ever falsified a time card or an expense report? If through a computer error you were given too large a paycheck, would you report it? Do you see such moral choices as black-and-white issues?

170

Most people say if they found a wallet full of cash on the street they would return the money; do you believe them? Most also think their own lost wallets would not be returned; do you feel similarly? How do you explain this contradiction? Would you help fund an experiment designed to find out whether people are actually honest enough to return cash-filled wallets?

172

Are you able to separate sex from love? Could you be content satisfying your sexual needs from people other than your mate? When you think of sex, do you think of a broad range of touching, holding, and caressing, or mainly of sexual intercourse?

177

Is there anything anyone could have told you that would have made your first sexual experience better? Do you think you would be better off if you had waited longer to have sex? if you had started earlier? Was sex what you imagined it to be?

178

What if you had to choose the 10 people who would die? Would you rather have someone else in the group make the decision even though you might be picked to die?

180

If you were offered a much better job in another city and knew you would, over the years, drift away from your closest friend if you took it, would you go?

193

What would induce you to give up life as you know it and face the unknown? Were people in previous centuries more adventurous than we are today or was it simply harder to avoid risk and adventure? How much does affluence make people complacent and averse to risk?

200

What are you looking for when you converse with people? What kinds of things do you usually discuss? Are there other things that would be more interesting to you?

GREGORY STOCK received his doctorate in bio-physics from the Johns Hopkins University in 1977 and has published papers on bacterial motility, amphibian limb regeneration, laser light-scattering, and 3-dimensional computer reconstruction. He has also developed electronic-banking software for Citicorp and graduated as a Baker Scholar from the Harvard Business School. He is now writing another book and doing research related to non-profit foundations.